Contents

The meaning of the words in **bold** can be found in the glossary.

pets and wild rodents

Pet rats and mice are the same as wild rats and mice but they are specially **bred** to be kept at home.

Rats and mice

Rats and mice are **rodents**, just like squirrels, hamsters and prairie dogs. All rodents have extra-large **gnawing** teeth at the front of their mouth, which continue to grow throughout their life. Both rats and mice are covered in fur apart from their tails and feet. Rats and mice are very similar but rats are bigger than mice.

▲ Pet mice (above) and rats (below) are the same size and shape as wild mice and rats.

Fancy friends

Pet rats and mice are called '**fancy**' rats and mice. They look much the same as those living in the wild but come in many more colours and hair types. For example, there are dark blue, lilac, silver and even red pet mice. Their fur can be one colour or several colours and it may be smooth, shiny, curly or long. However, pet rats and mice share many features with their wild cousins and if they escape they can happily live in the wild.

▶ Wild rats like this one (right) are either plain brown or black but fancy rats (below) have fur in a variety of colours and patterns.

Why a rat or mouse?

Rats and mice make great pets. They are fun, active animals that will get to know you and enjoy playing and learning tricks.

Perfect pet

Rats and mice make good pets because they don't take up too much space, they like to play and are fun to watch. But they do need daily care. Rats especially need lots of attention. They do not like being left in their cage all day.

Where to buy your pet

The best place to buy your pet is from a **breeder** of fancy mice and rats. A breeder will have spent time handling the pets so that they are used to people and less likely to bite. Also a breeder will be able to guide you on what type of pet to buy.

▲ A good breeder will help you choose a friendly pet and advise you on how to look after it and handle it.

Social animals

Pet rodents are **social** animals that like to live in groups. They like to **groom** each other and cuddle together to sleep, so you need to keep two or more animals of the same sex. Sometimes males fight, so two female mice or rats are better for first-time pet owners. A single mouse or rat will get lonely.

PET POINT
Young rats or mice should be at least 5 weeks old before they leave their mother.

▼ These pet mice are cuddling up in a group.

Choosing your pet

Rats and mice look similar, but there are differences that you need to think about before you buy your pet.

Large or small

Rats are bigger than mice and need a larger cage, which is more costly. They eat more food, too. But because they are bigger, rats are easier to handle than mice.

Are they friendly?

Both rats and mice can be trained to come out of their cage and play with you. Rats can be friendlier and are happy to sit on your shoulder or lap. Mice like to run around.

▼ A mouse can be tricky to handle at first as it is small and moves quickly.

▲ Your pet rat will enjoy being out of its cage and spending some time with you.

Rats need play

Rats are **intelligent** pets that like to explore and they need more attention than a mouse. Rats should not be left in their cage all day long and need at least an hour of play a day. If you cannot spare this amount of time then perhaps a rat is not for you.

Are they smelly pets?

Both rats and mice produce smelly wee (**urine**), but the wee of mice has a stronger smell. Male rats smell more than female rats because they spread little drops of wee around in their cage. Rats in the wild do this to mark their **territory**.

Preparing a new home

Once you have decided on whether to have rats or mice, you need to buy a cage and get ready for their arrival.

Large cage

Rats and mice do not like living outdoors. They need to be kept inside. Rats are active animals so buy as large a cage as possible.

A large wire cage with a **nest box** and solid floor is best for a rat. The solid floor stops their feet from getting stuck, and the wire sides are used for climbing. Mice can be kept in cages, too, but make sure the bars are close together so they cannot escape or get stuck. If you buy a wheel for your pet make sure it's a pet-safe design because poor designs can trap their feet and tail.

◀ Buy a wheel like this that has a solid running surface to stop your pets from being injured.

Interesting home

The best place to put your pets' cage is in a room where they can see lots of things going on. In the wild rats and mice run through pipes and climb up walls, so add things to make their cage interesting, such as shelves, ropes, ladders, old cardboard boxes and tubes.

▲ These rats have a lot of toys in their cage to keep them active.

Do it!

Checklist — things you will need for your new pets:

- cage
- selection of ropes and shelves for inside the cage
- water bottle
- food bowl
- toys
- bedding
- litter
- wood chew

Bedding

You need to put **litter** such as wood shavings or shredded recycled paper on the cage floor to **absorb** their urine and **droppings**. They need some soft paper in their nest box, too. Rats and mice love to shred bits of paper for their nest.

Caring for your pet

There are some basic rules for looking after your pet. Remember you need to check your pet every day.

Fresh water

Rats and mice need to have water available all the time. Drip-feed plastic bottles are easy to fill and do not spill water everywhere. Some rats like to have a bowl of water to wash themselves.

▶ Use a proper water bottle that fits safely on your pets' cage so they can reach it.

Do it!

Make sure your pets have fresh water every day. Once a week remove the water bottle and give it a clean with soapy water.

Cleaning

Replace your pets' litter and bedding once or twice a week to stop their cage getting smelly. Give the whole cage a really good clean every few weeks. Put your pets in a small plastic fish tank or something similar while you clean their cage. Make sure the lid has **air holes** or ask an adult to put some holes in the lid.

▲ Wear plastic gloves when you clean your pets' cage and always wash your hands well afterwards.

Grooming

Mice and rats are very clean animals and each day they spend a lot of time grooming themselves. Some of the long-haired mice can be brushed to stop their hair from getting tangled.

Handling your pet

Rats and mice soon get used to being handled. The more you handle them, the more they enjoy it.

Gentle handling

Your new pet may already be used to being handled. But most have never been picked up, so they may not like it at first. Talk to your pet softly so it gets to know your voice. Remember rats and mice are small animals and it is easy to scare them or injure them if you handle them roughly.

Picking up rodents

The best way to hold your pet is to pick it up around its chest with one hand. Place the other hand under its hind feet to support its back legs.

▲ Always support your pet's back legs; don't let them dangle.

Wriggling pets

Take care when getting your pet, especially a mouse, out of its cage as they could slip out and escape. When you have your pet in your hand, watch it carefully in case it tries to jump and get away. If your pet struggles and gets stressed when it's picked up, put it back in its cage.

PET POINT
Never pick up your pet by the end of its tail as this can cause injury.

▶ When your pet mouse gets to know you it will enjoy running about on your shoulders.

Wild Cousins

Wild rodents are more active at night. They clamber up trees and fences, **burrow** in the ground and chew wood.

Chewing

Both pet and wild rodents chew. They use their long **incisors** to chew through wood, wire and lots of other things. In the wild, rodents can do a lot of damage around farms where they chew through wooden doors to get at food stores.

Chew toys

The gnawing teeth of rodents grow throughout their life. They have to chew to wear them down, otherwise they become too long and they cannot eat properly. Pet rodents need toys such as blocks of wood that they can chew.

◀ In the wild, rats chew tree bark to keep their teeth short (left). Buy a special wood chew for your pets (below) to keep their teeth healthy.

Climbing experts

All rodents are good at climbing. In the wild they climb up rope, and clamber over plants and fences. They use their long tail to help grip and balance. Pet rodents will climb up the wires of their cage as well as furniture and curtains.

Do it!

Spot your pet's wild ways. When your pet is exploring a room, it will usually run along the floor near the wall and look for hiding places and food. In the wild, a rodent will stick close to trees or walls and not go out into open countryside where it could be caught by **predators**.

▲ Pet rats (top) and wild harvest mice (above) use their tail to help them balance when they climb.

The hunt for food

Rodents eat lots of different foods, in fact they will eat almost anything. This is why they are such successful animals in the wild.

Searching for food

Lots of rats and mice live on farms where they steal food put down for chickens and get into **grain stores**. Rats and mice can also cause problems in towns and cities where they feed on any waste food that is lying around or break into rubbish bags left on the street. Sometimes they enter homes and businesses in search of food.

◀ Both wild (above) and pet rats (left) love to eat wheat and other seeds.

Hiding food

Often wild rats and mice carry food to hiding places where they store it to eat later. They like to eat out of sight so that predators, such as birds and foxes, can't see them. Pet mice often hide their food, too, and eat it at night when it is quiet.

▼ This pet rat has its food in a sturdy bowl so the food doesn't spill out.

Feeding your pet

Both rats and mice eat a mix of foods such as vegetables and fruits, seeds and even bits of meat or dog food. An adult rat should be fed about a handful of dried food a day with a couple of teaspoons of fruit or vegetables. A mouse should be fed half this amount.

Training your pet

Rats and mice are very intelligent. With a little patience you will be able to train your pet to do all sorts of tricks.

Tricks

You can easily train your pet to come out of its cage when you call it or train it to find food in your pocket. Use food such as sunflower seeds as a reward when your pet does as you want. If you are training your pet, try not to feed it before training so that it is hungry and will be keen to find the food.

▼ You can use food treats to train your pet to come out of its cage.

Sit!

Train your pet to sit when you lift your finger up. Raise your finger up and at the same time hold a treat in front of your pet's nose. Slowly move the food up until the pet is sitting. You may have to repeat this many times but soon your pet will sit every time you lift your finger.

▲ Use food treats to train your pet mouse to stand up or sit.

PET POINT

Rodents can easily get fat, so do not give them too many fatty treats. A fat pet is less active and not as healthy.

Mazes

In the wild, rodents spend hours hunting for food and then have to remember the way home! See how good your pet is at finding its way around by building a simple **maze** in a small shoe box using bits of card to make the passages. Rats will use their excellent sense of smell to find their way through the maze to the food. If your rat has problems at first, move the food nearer to it.

Giving birth

In the wild, female rats and mice can have babies every month. Within a year they can produce 150 or more babies.

Nesting

A female rat or mouse makes a soft nest for her babies with shredded paper or old bits of cloth. Newborn rats and mice have pink skin with no hair. Their eyes are closed and their ears are stuck down. After 4 or 5 days hairs start to grow and the ears open. After two weeks their eyes open and they start to explore. Young rats and mice are ready to leave their mother and look after themselves when they are about 5 weeks old.

▲ This pet mouse (left) has a special nest box with shredded paper while the field mouse (right) makes a nest from bits of grass and straw.

Rat life cycle

A female rat or mouse is ready to breed at just 5 weeks but most people do not breed their rats until they are 6 months old and their mice until they are 3 months old. The female rat or mouse is **pregnant** for about 20 days and gives birth to as many as 18 babies, called kittens. Newborn rats and mice feed on their mother's milk until they are about 3 weeks old. Rats are fully grown by about 6 months. A pet rat can live for up to 3 years. A pet mouse for 1–2 years.

newborn rats

2-week-old babies

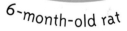
6-month-old rat

Play fighting

Young rats and mice chase and jump on top of each other. This is called play fighting and it stops when they are about a month old.

▲ In the wild the rats at the bottom of the pile are less likely to be caught by predators.

PET POINT

If your pet has babies, make sure you separate the males from the females when they are 4 weeks old otherwise you may end up with even more babies!

23

Rodent talk

Rodents communicate and find their way around using their senses, especially smell, sound and touch.

Using senses

Rodents cannot see as well as people but they have great hearing, smell and touch.

A rat's hearing is so good that if it was in the same room as you, it could hear you rubbing your finger and thumb together.

▲ Rats can hear **high-pitched** sounds that we cannot.

PET POINT
Some rats wiggle their tail when they get excited or when they are about to start a fight.

Alarm calls

When rodents are alarmed or distressed they make very high-pitched squeaks and shrieks that act as an alarm to others. When stressed they **grind** their teeth.

Whiskers

Rats and mice have long, stiff hairs called **whiskers** on their snout. They move them back and forth, brushing them over objects close to their face. This gives them a 'map' of their surroundings and helps them to find their way around. They also use their whiskers to feel other rodents.

▶ The pet mouse (right) and the wild mouse (below) are using their whiskers to check if they can squeeze through a hole. If their whiskers get through the hole the rest of their body will fit.

Smells

Rats and mice smear their urine on surfaces over which they walk. This leaves a trail of smells to help them find their way around. It is also a means of communicating with other rodents.

Instant expert

Rodents are found almost everywhere. Rats have been carried by ships to all parts of the world, apart from Antarctica, and some islands.

The biggest ...

The largest rodent is the capybara of South America. It weighs up to 70 kg. The largest true rat, related to the rats found in our towns and cities, was discovered in 2009. It was living in a **remote** jungle in Papua New Guinea. It was the size of a cat, about 1.5 kg in weight and 82 cm long.

FAST FACTS

Mice have nails on each of their toes that help them to grip when they climb.

▶ The capybara lives near water. They have slightly webbed feet and are excellent swimmers.

... and the smallest

The smallest mouse is the African pygmy mouse, just 8 to 10 cm long and weighing only 7 g.

An adult male rat weighs up to 700 g, females weigh a bit less.

◀ Pet mice give birth to between 10 and 20 young but really big **litters** can have up to 30 young.

Lots of pinkies

Baby mice are nicknamed pinkies because of their pink appearance. A male mouse is called a buck and a female a doe.

The Black Death

The **Black Death** swept across Europe during the 14th century and killed many millions of people. People thought it was brought by rats, but it was actually caused by the **fleas** carried by rats.

pet quiz

Now you know a bit more about what is involved in looking after rodents, is a mouse or rat the right pet for you?

1. **Do you know how much time you will need to take care of your pet each day?**
- **a)** Not sure
- **b)** I don't have any time to look after them
- **c)** At least an hour a day

2. **How long can rats live?**
- **a)** Not very long
- **b)** About 10 years
- **c)** About 3 years

3. **What type of housing is best for a rat?**
- **a)** A rabbit hutch
- **b)** An old fish tank
- **c)** A large wire cage with a solid floor

4. **At what age is a female rat ready to have babies?**
- **a)** 12 months
- **b)** 6 months
- **c)** 1 month

5. **When you go on holiday, what should you do with your pet?**
- **a)** Put out lots of food for it
- **b)** Keep it in its cage until we get back
- **c)** Ask a friend or family member to look after it

See page 32 to find out if a rat or mouse is the right pet for you.

Owning a pet — checklist

All pets need to be treated with respect. Remember, your pet can feel pain and distress – it is not a toy.

To be a good pet owner you should remember these five rules. Make sure your pet:

- never suffers from fear and distress
- is never hungry or thirsty
- never suffers discomfort
- is free from pain, injury and disease
- has the freedom to show its normal behaviour

This means you have to check your pet every day to make sure it has enough fresh water and food. You must keep its home clean and make sure that your pet has enough room to move around.

You must remember to order new supplies of its food in plenty of time so that your pet never goes hungry.

If your pet becomes ill or hurts itself you must take it to a vet to be checked over.

Unless you want your pet to have lots of babies, make sure you only keep rats or mice of the same sex together.

If you have other pets you must make sure they cannot harm or frighten your pet mouse or rat.

When you let your pet out to play, make sure the area is safe – that there is nothing sharp that can injure your pet, no wires for it to chew, or any plants that it might eat that are poisonous.

Glossary

absorb to soak up

air holes small holes in the lid of a box or container that let air in so the animal inside can breathe

Black Death also called the plague, a disease carried by fleas, tiny blood-sucking animals, living on rats. During the 14th century, the disease spread across Europe killing millions of people

bred reproduced, raised

breeder a person who keeps animals, such as pet rodents, to breed and sell

burrow to dig a hole, tunnel or shelter in the ground

droppings the solid waste that passes out from an animal's gut, also called faeces

fancy (rats and mice) animals that are bred to be colourful or attractive, rather than plain like a wild rat or mouse

flea small, blood-sucking insect that lives on other animals and can jump many times its own body length

gnawing chewing

grain stores places where large amounts of seeds, especially wheat, are stored

grind to rub together

groom to keep hair clean

high pitched a sound that is shrill or squeaky

incisor a type of tooth found at the front of the mouth of a rodent that never stops growing

intelligent able to understand and to learn

litter group of baby rats or mice born at the same time to the same mother

litter a material such as wood shavings or newspaper put on the bottom of a cage to help keep it clean

maze a system of paths or tunnels in which it is easy to get lost

nest box a place where rats and mice sleep and raise their young

predator an animal that hunts and eats other animals

pregnant when a female animal is carrying babies in her body

remote far away from people

rodent an animal that has large gnawing teeth, such as a rat

social animals that like to live with other animals of the same type

territory a particular place or area where a group of animals lives

urine liquid waste produced by the body of an animal, often called pee or wee

whiskers stiff hairs found around the nose, that are used for touch

Index

Pet quiz - results

If you answered (c) to most of the questions then a mouse or a rat could be for you.